1 John

A Question Driven Bible Study

JACOB TOMAN

Jacob Toman has been serving in ministry through leadership and preaching since 2009. He currently serves as the Pastor at Ada Christian Reformed Church. He has his Masters of Divinity from Covenant Theological Seminary and has served in the PCA, Non-Denomination and Reformed Churches. Jacob is married to Amy and they have 4 living children.

You can find more of Jacob's writings at Redeemingfamily.com. His sermons can be seen at Redeeming Family Youtube, just use the QR code below.

Redeeemingfamily.com

Podcast

Table of Contents

Forward

This study is intended for individuals, families, and groups who want to dive deeper into God's word. This is NOT an expository study but instead, it is a study that looks at how all of scripture works together. 1 John is a book that all Christians should study. This study can be used by new Christians and long-time Christians. Each week has 4 days of lessons that revolve around a passage in 1 John. In those 4 days, you will look at how scripture answers various questions that appear in 1 John. At the end of each lesson, there are additional resources for the catechisms and YouTube videos.

1 John is broken into smaller groupings to follow an exegetical outline. By studying each major idea communicated in the text, we will see both the individual assertions and collective whole assertions of 1 John.

The questions herein primarily originate from several seasons in life where I have personally grown in faith considering God's Word from 1 John. Everywhere the Lord sends me, this book has been of tremendous use. From my early days of ministry serving in a local church, 1 John was the focus of Bible study groups I was tasked to lead by my local pastor.

During my early days as a seminary student, I learned Biblical Greek by translating all of 1 John from Greek to English. Then later on in life, 1 John has been the focus of exegetical papers, doctrinal debates, small group presentations, Bible studies, personal evangelism, public apologetics, Sunday school classes, and sermon series. 1 John has never been far from me in the work Christ has called me to in service to His kingdom.

Why is this little epistle so applicable and beneficial to Christians today? Because the hike we are on can be treacherous. The dangers in the Christian race of faith abound. Such dangers like temptation to bitterness, indwelling sin, quarrelsome conflict, doubt of God's goodness, doubt of our position before God, uncertainty about God's message and God's messengers, distinguishing between true teaching and false teaching, and persevering while suffering. These are all topics addressed in some way within 1 John that we all as believers in Christ will most certainly encounter for ourselves, or among brothers and sisters in Christ.

As comforting, challenging, and helpful as 1 John has been to me, and to others whom I have served in the name of Jesus, I hope it is for you. May the Lord bless you, equipping you with the truth of 1 John for the life of faith in Christ

Background on 1 John

One of the unique aspects of John as a person was the period of time over which we see his faith lived out. While some New Testament writers were inspired by God to contribute a single letter to the New Testament (like James, Jude, Matthew, and Mark) John was inspired to contribute multiple writings over multiple decades. While the Apostle Paul was used by God to write the greatest number of New Testament letters, John was used by God to write over the longest period of time and a wide variety of genres. Throughout church history the Apostle John is believed to have written: The Gospel of John, 1 John, 2 John, 3 John, and Revelation.

John lived through the events he witnessed in the Gospel of John. John references this very emphatically in 1 John 1. As a young man John and his brother James, both followed Jesus (Mark 1:19-20). As a middle-aged man, John witnessed the rapid spread of the Gospel to various regions surrounding the Mediterranean. As an older man, John was tasked with sharing the overwhelming good news of Christ Jesus' ultimate triumph over sin and death, redeeming a people for Himself for joy unending into eternity.

John came from a family of workers. He would have been "blue collar". John was just a dude learning the family business (Matthew 4:21-22). John wasn't qualified to become a follower of Jesus because of his own goodness, educational background, or past accomplishments. John was qualified to follow Jesus because Christ called him to follow. You and I can take comfort in that the same gospel John shared, is the same gospel that calls us to follow Christ. In this way, you and I, regardless of our backgrounds, cultures, family lineage, or language, share a mutual common reality. We have heard the gospel and are responding in faith to Christ's magnificent redeeming work. John's life of faith calls us away from all that we would say is religious, dramatic, and dogmatic about ourselves apart from Christ.

John's life testifies to something beyond human-originated concepts of religion, tradition, and ordinances. John's writings and life testifies to the Divine Truth, to God Incarnate, and to the maker of all creation taking on Body and Blood. John's gospel, his letters to churches, and his prophecy all point to the most dramatic reality that defines each and every person for all eternity: Christ's life, death, resurrection, ascension, reign, and return.

Pre- Study

Before beginning your studies, let me for a moment challenge you to engage in some "pre-study" reading. Read through the whole of 1 John before you engage in your deeper study of individual passages. I have benefited tremendously from reading large chunks of scripture.

It may take you somewhere between 15-20 minutes to read the whole of 1 John. These are 15-20 minutes that are incredibly well spent as they will shape your appreciation and understanding of the text for the rest of your study. Imagine for a moment reading only a single sentence of a multi page letter from a dear loved one. Would you know the depth of your loved ones' communication well from only a single sentence? Perhaps you are trying to learn a new skill and are therefore reading a guidebook. Would you be able to gain mastery of the skill by only reading the guidebook through the first paragraph? It is a poor habit indeed when we approach the sacred scriptures of God's revealed Word and think that a mere drop of a few words will be transformational in our lives.

I remember chatting with a wise older pastor who had long served the Lord. He shared his testimony of conversion by stating that despite working in many Christian private schools, he was not converted until many years of marriage. He shared that he often throughout his life had "read" the Bible, but he had not "searched" the Bible. He had "read" the Bible, but he had not delved into the scriptures with curiosity, longing, and love for the Lord who inspired the Bible. After being converted, the man spent years searching the Bible, learning to re-read the Bible with new affections, and new ambitions.

Take this pre-study challenge as an opportunity to search the scriptures with curiosity, longing, and love that doesn't stop with a short verse or two. Read the whole of 1 John and begin to see the whole letter as it was initially composed by the Inspired Biblical author under the guidance of the Holy Spirit.

For more teaching scan the QR Code for a 1 John sermon for each Lesson.

Lesson 1
Seen, Heard, & Touched

Read 1 John 1

Day 1: The Apostle John was used mightily by the Lord to write the Gospel of John, 3 small letters (called epistles), and the book of Revelation. In these various sacred, inspired portions of God's Word, we get a glimpse of John at various life stages and circumstances. Of all the New Testament writers, John is perhaps the most diverse in the style and genre of communication he was tasked by the Lord to write.

Who was the Apostle John according to the following passages?

Mark 1:19-20

Luke 5:10

Mark 10:35

Mark 3:17

Day 2: John was writing this book to a group of churches where fellowship with each other was at stake. For the believer who has been redeemed by Christ, fellowship is not a result of any earthly category or connection. Christians are not connected because of mutually shared political beliefs, upbringing, language, culture, financial status, or favorite food. We are connected because we are one in Christ. The Son of God has brought into union all who are, by grace, elected to eternal life. It is a noble and worthwhile aim and desire as Christians to be in mutual fellowship with one another. For the Apostle John, there was no such thing as a solitary, lone-ranger Christian. Christians are in union together because every true Christian is united to Christ. Through Christ, we are one.

In the following passages, what do you observe about the fellowship of believers?

Acts 16:31-34

Acts 2:42-47

1 Peter 4:7-10

Philippians 2:1-4

Day 3: John's focus of this book was on what he had seen, heard, and touched. John was writing about something that is very real. He is using language to describe what is real. He does not discuss religious philosophy or make an argument about religious teachings. He was writing about very real experiential stuff that he had heard, seen, and touched.

What words does John use in 1 John 1:1-4 to convey his tangible experience with the Lord?

1 John 1:1-4

In what way were senses (taste, touch, hearing, sight, smell) tangibly described in the following passages?

Luke 2:15

Matthew 7:24-27

Luke 24:36-44

Day 4: We can see in 1 John 1:1-4 the importance of the proclamation of the gospel. This proclamation by John occurs so that believers may have complete Joy in Christ.

What do you observe from these passages that speak about Joy?

Philippians 2:1-4

Acts 5:17-42

Psalm 30

Digging Deeper

Take a look at the confession, or catechism that your church follows. What does it have to say about having complete joy in Christ?

Heidelberg Catechism Questions: 1,2,5, 55.

Westminster Catechism 1,2, 88.

The 1689 London Baptist Confession Chapter 17,27.

How does the Joy of Christ take shape in your life? When have there been tangible moments of the Joy of Christ in your life?

Lesson 2
Getting Scammed

Read 1 John 1:5-2:2

Day 1: John had learned that some churches, whom he loves, were getting scammed. They are being taught falsely! Instead of being built up and taught in the things of Christ that lead to joy, the churches were being swindled out of their joy! John is here to expose these lies and correct what has been wrongly taught. These churches were being taught scams about God's character. This is nothing new to Christians. God, in His mercy, has blessed us with corrective instructions (like here in the book of 1 John) to avoid being scammed by false teaching. Much of the world today claims God is either evil or that God is hidden. These claims are clearly opposed in the Word of God. Christ Jesus is God revealed in the flesh.

What do we see about God's character in the following passages?

1 John 1:5

John 3:16-21

Hebrews 1:1-3

Isaiah 40:21-31

Day 2: : In 1 John 1:8-9 we see two claims that John makes about sin; to be "without sin" and that "we have not sinned". To be "without sin" today translates to "to be basically good". The second claim "we have not sinned" is rebellion against God during life. These were two lies, and two scams that are still present today. John corrects both of these lies with encouragement found in verse 9.
What do these verses say about sin?

Romans 3:23

1 Corinthians 15:1-3

Romans 6:23

Ephesians 2:1-10

Day 3: In John's day there were scams about getting right with God. One scam that has occurred throughout church history is the scam of penance. Some have taught that if you sin against God, you must do some great work to make up for that sin. Brothers and sisters, hear the good news of the Gospel! The bad news of the gospel is that we in ourselves could never make up for our sins. The good news of the Gospel is that the only one who could take the complete penalty for our sins has done so! Christ lived the perfect life, died the atoning death we deserved as sinners, rose again from the dead, and ascended into heaven triumphantly glorified before God the Father.

What do the following passages say about salvation from sin and the wrath of God against sin?

Romans 1:18-22

1 Peter 2:21-25

Ephesians 5:1-20

Day 4: The last scam is about the reach of Christ's atoning work. During the first century, after Jesus' resurrection and ascension, some were teaching that Christ's saving work was only available to certain people groups. Throughout time and history, many have claimed you need to do this, you need to be in this place, a part of this group, a doer of these things, you need to have this skin color, you need to have these parents or grandparents to be saved by Christ. These are all scams. Christ's atoning sacrificial work is available to every type of person, regardless of demographic qualifiers. As the folk song goes "Red and yellow, black and white, they are precious in his sight". The only thing that keeps people from receiving the benefits of Jesus' atoning work is a rejection of Christ.

According to these verses, who has Christ come to save?
Luke 19:1-10

Matthew 1:18-25

1 Timothy 1:15-17

Digging Deeper

Take a look at the confession, or catechism that your church
follows. What does it say about Salvation?

Heidelberg Catechism: Questions 4 and 30.

Westminster Shorter Catechism Questions 86-91.

London Baptist Confession Chapter 15.

What are some sins you can with thankfulness and joy praise God
for redeeming you from? How would you describe the forgiveness of
God to someone who doesn't yet know Jesus?

Lesson 3
Knowing God

Read 1 John 2:3-11

Day 1: How do we become assured and confident that we believe and know God? We grow in our assurance and confidence that we know God because of growing love, obedience, and trust in God. John emphasizes that our love, obedience, and belief give confidence and assurance that we are in reality new creations, God's people, God's dearly beloved adopted children.

How would you describe the relationship between obedience and knowing God in the following passages?

John 17:1-8

2 Corinthians 4:13-16

Acts 26:1-23

Day 2: John has no problem calling out people who claim to know God, but do not live following him. Confrontation sometimes must occur. God's Word calls out that a life lived in opposition to God, is not a life lived in love with God. Walking as Jesus walked means we are to love, be obedient to God, and conduct ourselves with proper humility. Jesus loved the Lord his God and Father and his neighbor as himself. He lived in perfect obedience, submitting to the will of God the Father. His life was marked by selfless humility believing God's plan was best.

In what ways are we called to humble ourselves in submission to God?
James 4:4-10

1 Peter 4:1-6

Philippians 2:1-13

Day 3: Often in the days of the Old Testament, God gave previews, sometimes called "shadows" about the great Redeemer who was to come (Matthew 4:16, Colossians 2:17, Hebrews 8:5; 10:1). John's audience was familiar with the Old Testament. They knew about the "old commandment" (1 John 2:7). John was writing to his audience about how Christ was the full revelation of God. This is John's way of saying "Hey, I'm not writing to you about the Old Testament and the Old Ways, I'm writing to you about the one whom the Old Testament was about! The one who makes God fully known". The person of Christ answers so many questions about who God is, His plans, His character, and His purposes. John saw a unity between the Old Testament and the life of Christ.

What does the New Testament have to say about Christ as a fulfillment of ancient scriptures?

1 Corinthians 15:1-4

Matthew 1:1-18

Mark 1:1-15

Day 4: Knowing God through love isn't just conceptual awareness. Biblical knowledge means "being on the same page", "having unity", "growing closer", and "becoming more like the other". To love one another is to live in the light. To hate your brother or sister is to live in the darkness

How does the Bible give tangible examples of how we are to Love God?

Luke 10:25-37

Deuteronomy 6:4-13

John 14:22-24

Matthew 6:1-15

Digging Deeper

Take a look at the confession, or catechism that your church

follows. What does it say about God?

Heidelberg Catechism: Questions 4,5, 26.

Westminster Shorter Catechism Questions 1, 2, 4,5,6.

1689 London Baptist Confession Chapter 2.

What about God's character is lovable? What is attractive about

who God is?

Lesson 4
A Reason and A Worry

Read 1 John 2:12-17

Day 1 : John writes that forgiveness from God and knowing God are two of the hallmarks of early Christian life. When God through the Holy Spirit makes us aware of our sin before God and our status as guilty rebels, we then recognize our great and perilous need for mercy. As guilty rebels, we are in need of forgiveness. One of the first early experiences in the believer's life is forgiveness of sins.
How do the following passages speak about forgiveness?
Acts 2:36-41

Hebrews 9:22

Matthew 26:28

Acts 10:39-43

Day 2: John speaks of the mature Christians; those who have been through much, and grown much in the Lord. A father is someone who has contributed to anothers life. This is precisely the role John uses to describe this group, this group as "fathers". This group of "mature" Christians has been a "father" to other Christians. They have made disciples and taught others what was taught to them. This group is made up of those who have experienced the Christian life and put to use what they have received from God in training others toward godliness

What are the practices and disciplines you observe in the following passages about believers growing in faith?

Luke 24:13-35

Acts 4:1-4

Acts 19:1-10

Romans 6:17

Philippians 3:15-21

Day 3: John addresses a group in the churches that he calls "young men" in verses 13 and 14. This is a group who are in the thick of the Christian life's struggles. Those who are continually experiencing the tensions of old sin and new life through Christ. For this group spiritual warfare isn't a concept, it's a daily reality. This group is continually overcoming. Overcoming sin through growing in strength in the Lord. Growing because the Word of God lives within them.

How would you describe how Joseph and David resisted temptation in the midst of an opportunity to sin?

Genesis 39:1-17

1 Samuel 24:1-22

Day 4: John gives a warning in verse 15, "15 Do not love the world or anything in the world. If anyone loves the world, love for the Father is not in them." The world is in contrast to the Father. Love of the world is not love of the father. The world here doesn't mean the earth, the material realm, or creation. We know this because John gives us a definition of what he's writing about in verse 16: "For everything in the world the lust of the flesh, the lust of the eyes, and the pride of life—comes not from the Father but from the world".

What strategies do the following passages give for dealing with temptation?

1 Corinthians 10:13

2 Timothy 2:22

1 Peter 5:8-9

Digging Deeper

Take a look at the confession, or catechism that your church follows. What does it say about sin?

Heidelberg Catechism Questions 6,7,8.

Westminster Shorter Catechism Question 14.

1689 Baptist Confession Chapter 6.

What are some temptations you are learning to struggle against? How have you seen or heard others learn to struggle well against their temptations?

Lesson 5
Do Not Be Led Astray

Read 1 John 2:18-27

Day 1: John begins by speaking of the dear children of God. These children have heard and know the truth of Christ. Because the audience knows the truth, John writes to them (v21) See that what you have heard from the beginning remains in you.

What do these passages have to say about listening from the beginning?

Hebrews 2:1-4

Colossians 3:1-4

Luke 1:1-4

Day 2: The dear children are in contrast with the Antichrist. Some throughout history have thought of the Antichrist as a singular person or symbolic figure of the far-distant future. John wrote about the spirit of the Antichrist in the present tense. There were those who qualified as Antichrist in the very beginning days of the church.

How do these passages describe the Antichrist?

2 John 1:7

1 John 4:3

1 John 2:22

Day 3: John writes with a repeated emphasis on the connection of God the Son and God the Father. A clear contrast is spoken between those who remain faithful to the truth about Christ, and those who have abandoned the truth and left the church. For John, the relationship between the Son and the Father is an essential part of Christian belief.

How do these other passages speak about the relationship of God the Son and God the Father?

John 5:16-30

John 17:1-19

Colossians 1:15-20

Day 4: There is a clear contrast between what is true and what is false throughout this letter. The writer earnestly desires for his audience to be able to distinguish between what is of Christ (true) and what is of the Antichrist (untrue). Throughout the New Testament, faithfulness to Christ was often known through testimony given about the person and work of Jesus.

How do these passages speak about the person and work of Jesus?

Hebrews 1:1-4

Romans 5:15-17

1 Peter 3:15-22

Digging Deeper

Take a look at the confession, or catechism that your church follows. What does it say about salvation?

Heidelberg Catechism Questions 61,62,63,64.

Westminster Shorter Catechism Question 87,94.

1689 Baptist Confession Chapter 18.

What are some ways you have seen God's Salvation in your life?

Lesson 6
Children of God

Read 1 John 2:28-3:6

Day 1: As Christians, we are called Children of God. We are children of God because of a change that has happened. For a person to change from being a child of the world to being a child of God there is an essential change that must occur. To be a child of God one must receive Christ. All those who are children of God are in that family due to God's mercy and grace. It was due to God's grace, mercy, and favor that we have been moved from a kingdom of darkness into the kingdom of God. John continually uses this phrase, throughout his letters "dear children" to address those whom he considers to be his children and to refer to God's people. We are not an extended family, we are the closest family. We are Children of God.

What do these passages say about the family of God?

John 1:12-13

Romans 8:12-17

Philippians 2:14-16

Day 2: There is much change that occurs when we become Christians and there is much change that will occur in our future. We know that when Christ appears again we shall be like him. Jesus was one whom John saw, heard, and touched. Jesus, both in his earthly life and in his resurrected life, was genuinely a person with flesh and bone. Jesus was truly physical in his resurrection. When Christ returns, we too will be truly physical in our resurrection. We shall be like him. We don't have all the details of what that change will look like in eternity, but we know it will be a real life. A physical life, with bodies that can touch and eat, and we know in that new life we will never again be stained by sin or any of its harms.

How does scripture speak about our sure hope of resurrection as physical beings?

John 20:24-29

1 Corinthians 15:35-58

John 21:15

1 John 3:2-3

Day 3: Christians are not perfect, but Christians live aiming towards Christ's perfection. Living a life pleasing to God (in conformity to God's revealed will through God's Word) is our aim daily. When the Christian is convicted of sin, the born-again Christian struggles against that sin. Sin for the Christian becomes something to overcome, fight against, struggle with, and wage war on. Sin isn't something that the Christian accepts. This is the change that we currently experience throughout our earthly lives as believers. We are living changed lives that are continually discovering more about our sin, and discovering more about our savior. People are always living in a manner that is growing. Either a person is growing in the practice of sin or is growing in the practice of faith in Christ.

What does the Bible tell us about how we are to change as we grow in faith?

Colossians 2:6-23

Hebrews 6:1-3

James 1:2-18

Day 4: Christians are people of change. Because of what has changed (we have been born again), what will change (we will be as Christ is when He appears), and what is changing in us during our earthly lives (through continued growth in the Christian life). Our faith is rooted in a God who does not change, and who has caused in us the greatest change possible - from spiritual death to new spiritual life!

Read through some of the ways the Bible speaks about sin, what are some of the sins the Lord is growing you to overcome and struggle against?

Exodus 20:1-17

1 Corinthians 6:1-20

Philippians 2:12-16

Digging Deeper

Take a look at the confession, or catechism that your church

follows. What does it say about children of God?

Heidelberg Catechism Questions 20,21,22,23,32.

Westminster Shorter Catechism Question 37,38,39.

1689 Baptist Confession Chapter 18.

Can you think of a time in your own life when you saw the results of

being a child of God? Have you seen changes in your life as you

become more like Christ?

Lesson 7
Love's Command & Example

Read 1 John 3:7-20

Day 1: Two families are put in contrast in this passage. The families are marked by what they continue in. The Children of God continue in faith and forsake sin. The children of God are marked by repentance - not just a single prayer or season of repentance, but continual repentance whenever sin is found. Faith in God grows through repentance and growth in obedience. The children of the Devil do not struggle against sin but instead continue in sin. Cain is given as the example of the children of the Devil, his way of living being a way of death. Christ is the ultimate example for the children of God, His way of living being the way of love.

How do the following passages demonstrate the love of Christ tangibly displayed?

Luke 5:12-32

Mark 8:22-33

Philippians 2:5-11

Day 2: Hatred is common in our world today. Turn on any news station and you see a world full of hate. It wasn't much different in John's time. Hatred is a family trait of fallen humanity. Hatred comes naturally. John demonstrates the example of hate with Cain and Abel. Notice that hatred is something that occurs within the bounds of a relationship.
How do these other biblical passages speak about hatred?

Matthew 6:19-24

Galatians 5:19-21

Romans 12:9-21

Day 3: Love is the opposite of hatred. John demonstrates the example of love for brother and sister in Christ. Christ laid down his life for us and we ought to lay down our lives for one another. Love is not abstract, love is not an emotion. Love is a concrete, tangible, actionable reality. Love is something that is expressed within a relationship. Love is pursuing the highest good and enjoyment of another. God provides for the highest good and enjoyment of His people by securing an eternally abundant life for his people. God's love abounds as His children love one another!

What does it look like for us to show love according to the following passages?

Mark 12:28-31

Philippians 2:1-4

Matthew 5:43-48

Day 4: John has put these tests before us; the test of faith (what we believe) and the test of life (what we do). These two tests grant us confidence that we are children of God. God knows who his children are, and lays out clearly, all throughout his Word what it means to be his children.

How does the Bible speak about the Christian's source of assurance that we belong to God?

Hebrews 11:1-12:13

2 Peter 1:3-11

Romans 5:1-11

Digging Deeper

Take a look at the confession, or catechism that your church

follows. What does it say about God's Love?

Heidelberg Catechism Questions 43, 45

Westminster Shorter Catechism Question 42, 90, 100, 101

1689 Baptist Confession Chapter 20

What are some ways that you can show God's love to others in your

life? How can you be sure of God's love for you?

Lesson 8
Confidence in Prayer

Read 1 John 3:21-24

Day 1: In this passage, we are shown how we might have confidence in prayer, even as we are encouraged and commanded to believe and to love. Our prayers are heard as they are offered up to God through Christ Jesus. Our beliefs are only true if they are founded on the One who is the Way, the Truth, and the Life. Our love is only pure if it is flowing from the one who is love: God himself.

How do these other biblical passages speak about the source of Christian confidence in prayer?

Romans 8:26-39

Matthew 6:5-8

Mark 11:24-26

Hebrews 4:14-16

Day 2: The Christian life is one of continually growing into Christ. We may not notice, or feel the change each moment, or each day, yet, by God's gracious work, we are growing more and more like Christ. John writes in 1 John 3:24 about how there is a new life the believer enjoys in God. The proposition is not a mistranslation or a mistake. The believer abides in God, and God abides within the believer.

What do these biblical passages speak about new life in Christ?

2 Corinthians 5:17

John 1:12

Colossians 3:9-10

Day 3: We are a part of God's kingdom. We are agents of God's kingdom. All that you are doing in your life is a part of God's work to build his kingdom. If you are a believer you are then an agent of God's kingdom work. All of history is moving towards a general direction of Christ's kingdom.

What do the following passages say about God's kingdom?

Matthew 13:31-32

1 Chronicles 29:11

Romans 14:7

Day 4: When we pray "thy will be done" we are recognizing God's will. We are submitting for God's will to be accomplished. We should live in sincere conviction and with the devoted determination that God's will is worth pursuing, knowing, learning, following, and then sharing. We should view ourselves as agents of God's will, not simply as passive bystanders.

What are some ways that you could live according to God's will?

1 Thessalonians 5:18

Luke 9:23

1 Peter 2:15

Digging Deeper:

Take a look at the confession, or catechism that your church follows. What does it say about prayer?

Heidelberg Catechism Question 46-52.

Westminster Shorter Catechism Question 98.

1689 Baptist Confession Chapter 22.

How do you pray in your own life? In what ways have you prayed for God's will and what was the outcome?

Lesson 9
Test the Spirits

Read 1 John 4:1-6

Day 1: John mentions in this passage two sorts of Spirits. He calls one the Spirit of God, and the other the spirit of the antichrist. He differentiates these spirits by their origin. One comes "from God", whereas the other is not from God but from the world. John again names these two spirits as the Spirit of Truth and the Spirit of falsehood.

What do these other biblical passages have to say about the Spirit of God?

John 14:15-21

1 Timothy 4:1

Deuteronomy 18:14-22

Day 2: John says do not believe every spirit. This means not trusting, or putting your confidence in, every Spirit. We could say don't trust everything you hear that sounds spiritual or religious. You must use discernment. The Christian ought to be skeptical and continually check what we believe with what God's Word has revealed. Our attitude even when we gather together on each Lord's day should not be "Oh well whatever so and so says is true, because I can trust so and so". Guess what, wolves wear sheep's clothing. They take time to deceive, they do their best to appear true and worthy of reception. So John warns us to be skeptical even when we think that the thing being taught or instructed is coming from a trusted source.

What are some characteristics of false teachers?
1 Timothy 6:3-5

Titus 1:10-16

Galatians 1:6-9

Day 3: The potential pitfalls of believing lies and rejecting the truth is that we will love the world instead of loving Christ. This has immediate and eternal ramifications. We will hate like Cain, rather than love like Christ. Ignorance and twisting of God's Word are two of the false teacher's greatest tools to deceive and sow evil. False teachers love for people to rely more on their thoughts than on God's Word to evaluate life. God loves his people and warns them how to be safeguarded from false teachings and teachers.

How can we be safeguarded from false teaching?

Ephesians 4:14-15

1 Thessalonians 5:19-22

Jude 4

Acts 20:28-32

Day 4: You cannot outsource Godliness. You must pick up God's Word, examine it, study it, and grow in your knowledge of it, otherwise, you may fall into false teaching and false religion. The relationship you have with God is not something someone else can live for you. John was very concerned for his audience that they would not fall for false religion. False religion does sometimes find its way into the community of believers. If it didn't, God wouldn't have inspired John to write this to a church! So please don't take offense when I say, we have aspects of false human religion even in our midst! We need to search the scriptures and use critical minds that are alert and seeking God's ways.

How can we be safeguarded from false teaching? How do these other passages speak against or about false teaching and false teachers?

Ezekiel 13:1-16

Revelation 2:18-28

2 Peter 1:12-21

1 Timothy 1:4-7

Digging Deeper

Take a look at the confession, or catechism that your church follows. What does it say about false teaching?

Heidelberg Catechism 19,21

Westminster Shorter Catechism Questions 55

1689 Baptist Confession Chapter 15

How can you be on the look out for false teaching? In what ways can you be an advocate against false teaching?

Lesson 10
Love Defined

Read 1 John 4:7-21

Day 1: Our beliefs are tied to our actions. The source of love will direct the destination of love. Love that springs out of faith in God cannot run out, but instead, abounds and overflows. The love of God is on display in the conduct of those who dwell in the love of God. The source and object of love are often revealed in action.

How do these passages speak about the source and object of our actions?

Matthew 12:22-37

Matthew 15:1-20

James 3:13-4:12

Day 2: Both the Bible and God's Word often speak of love. Love as the world speaks is often fleeting. The source of worldly love is worldly affection. Love as God's Word speaks is faithful and unswervingly committed. The source of Godly love is God. It was God's love motivating the sacrificial death of Jesus on the cross.

Worldly love is self-glorifying, divine love is God-glorifying. How do these passages describe different sorts of love?

Romans 5:6-11

1 Thessalonians 4:1-12

2 Timothy 3:1-5

Day 3: The love John writes about isn't something fickle, or fleeting. This love isn't limited to mortal conditions or circumstances like when we have had a great night's sleep, and our coffee, and are in a good mood. The love that John is speaking of, is a love that comes from God. John speaks about the love from God that comes from the very nature of God (God is love), which was revealed ultimately in the life and death of Christ Jesus.

This love is one of John's repeated themes throughout the whole book of 1 John. How do these other passages describe God's love?

Psalm 36:5-10

Psalm 118

Exodus 34:1-14

Day 4: John encourages the church to look at the cross and to love one another. Husbands are called to love their wives, as Christ loved the church. We are called to love one another as brothers and sisters. This kind of love does stuff, This love is actionable and it's personal. Love can't be spoken of without talking about a person. Love is a personal hing that people do. We can look to Christ to see the display of love in action. John urges his audience to love like Christ. This task by John is impossible for us on our own. The only way we can love one another according to God's word is to remember that God is love, and to love through God's love. We can only love like this because God is continually making us more like Jesus. Our love for one another has to come from God.

In what ways does God continually sanctify (grow) us to be more like Him in order to love one another?

2 Peter 1:3-11

1 Peter 4:1-11

Hebrews 13:1-8

Digging Deeper

Take a look at the confession, or catechism that your church follows. What does it say about sanctification?

Heidelberg Catechism Questions 20,21

Westminster Shorter Catechism Question 35

1689 Baptist Confession Chapter 13

Think over your life and write down some ways that you have grown in your Faith.

Lesson 11
Three Offensive Words

Read 1 John 5:1-12

Day 1: The Bible's call to believe is quite offensive to the world because it is authoritative, consequential, and exclusive. The call to believe is authoritative in that it is God our maker who calls us to believe in His son. It is consequential because there are both present and eternal consequences in our response to God's call to believe. And it is exclusive because this belief is rooted in what God has commanded us to believe. God's exclusive call to believe puts all other systems of belief on notice. God is not sneaky or deceptive about his revelation of truth. He has sent his prophets, revealed his Word, sent his Son, and continually provides for the proclamation of the exclusive truth.

What do these passages have to say about the authority of God's Word?

John 1:1-18

2 Timothy 3:14-16

Isaiah 40:8

Matthew 5:17-19

Day 2: The love the Bible speaks of is not the same thing as the love the world speaks of. By this point in our study of John, we've seen just how often stark contrasts and extreme comparisons are used to demonstrate the differences between God's ways and the ways of the world. The love that comes from God is not a roaming love, it's not a wandering love, it's not a carefree love. The love of God is a faithful love, a promise-keeping love, a care-filled love. The world as it loves is aimless, misguided, and casual. God is the one who ultimately defines what love is. The true revelation of love is love incarnate in Christ Jesus. That love is offensive to the lost world. Christ's love was not aimless. It was purposeful, intentional, and committed to the utmost.

In what ways do these passages speak of how Christians are instructed to daily live out the love of God?

Matthew 25:31-40

1 Corinthians 13:1-13

John 15:1-27

Ephesians 5:1-33

Day 3: Sinful humanity does not take kindly to overt calls to obey. For the sinful mind, the command to obey is burdensome. It is a weight, it is oppressive, it is a task, it is arduous, it is annoying, it is overwhelming. For the unbeliever the commands of God, the expectations of the creator are an unwelcome, unwanted nuisance. A call to obedience to the rebellious is seen as a threat and is responded to with arrogant defiance. Spiritually, God's commands are an impossibility to live up to for the unbeliever! Yet for the one who has in faith believed that Jesus is the Redeemer, the command to obey is something entirely different.

How does scripture speak of our ability to obey God or please him in our own efforts?

Ephesians 2:1-3

Jeremiah 17:5-11

Acts 17:16-34

Galatians 3:1-14

Day 4: For the believer in Christ who loves God, the call to obey comes as a victorious call to arms, rather than a burden. Overcoming the world is a tremendous display of power. It's not an attention-seeking self-display of power like what the world considers power. Instead, it is a selfless witness of a power that comes from beyond the individual. Worldly power consists of exercising force to achieve your own desires. The power of God is within the gospel for salvation from sin. The believer who has been redeemed by God overcomes the world, and this is victory, even our faith. Obedient living is victorious living. Obedience to God is life abundant.

How do these passages describe what it means to live a good life in relationship to God?

Psalm 119:1-16

Matthew 5:1-16

Matthew 11:25-30

Digging Deeper

Take a look at the confession, or catechism that your church follows. What does it say about obedience?

Heidelberg Catechism Questions 7,9,10,104,114

Westminster Shorter Catechism Question 12,39,40

1689 Baptist Confession Chapter 19

What are some ways that God has or is calling you to obey Him?

Lesson 12
The New Nature

Read 1 John 5:13-21

Day 1: God has given us a new nature. For those who have faith in Christ Jesus, there is a new love and a new obedience. This new nature informs our living. While we were yet sinners, we were uncertain of many things. We had no firm foundation for life, in our sin we were dead. But now that we are believers we have certainty about a great many things, one of which is eternal life. We know that we have eternal life. Just as Christ rose again from the grave to live and never die again, we too will rise from the grave to live and never die again.

What do these passages say about eternal life?

2 Corinthians 4:16-18

Romans 6:23

Revelation 21:3-4

John 17:1-5

1 Corinthians 15:1-58

Day 2: In addition to knowing that we have eternal life, John also writes that we know something about prayer because of our new nature and our new position as family members within God's family. We can have confidence in prayer. When the goals, efforts, and motivations of our hearts line up with God's heart, we can know God is at work bringing about what we ask. Prayer is not about convincing or changing God's mind. Prayer is not about bending the divine will to our will, prayer is about growing in our new affection for God such that His will becomes our will.

What can we learn about prayer from these passages?

1 Thessalonians 5:16-18

Matthew 6:5-15

James 5:13-16

Psalm 86:1-17

Day 3: Our certainty in prayer is contingent upon whether or not our prayers are in line with God's will. We know God's will by seeking him and considering what he has revealed in his word. God is not a hidden God, not a deceptive God. He is not a God who delights in concealing himself. God is light. God has revealed himself in his Son. God has spoken to his people through his prophets, through his word, through his Son, and through his Son's apostles. God's Word is revealed and demonstrated in the right preaching of the scriptures and in the right administration of the Sacraments.

How do these passages speak about God's will?
John 7:16-19

Colossians 4:12

Day 4: At the very end of this letter, John ends with a phrase that may seem detached or unrelated to the rest of the book. What do idols have to do with loving one another? As we've seen throughout our study of 1 Kohn, and many other passages, the true God has revealed himself. God is not a concept or an abstract religious construct. God is a being who has made Himself known to humanity via His Word and His Son Jesus. It makes sense then, after speaking of the awesome loving God, for John to give a very brief warning, almost like a parent giving final instructions to children. There are only two paths of pursuit in life, we will either remain steadfast in the love of God, or we will pursue idols. John lovingly reminds his audience which way of the two to go.

How do these passages speak of the danger of false gods, idols, and false worship?

1 Kings 11:1-13

Amos 5:18-27

Romans 1:18-32

Digging Deeper

Take a look at the confession, or catechism that your church follows. What does it say about God's Will?

Heidelberg Catechism Questions 89,90,94,96

Westminster Shorter Catechism Question 7,24,31

1689 Baptist Confession Chapter 3

Who is one person you know who you wished knew the love of God?

Study Epilogue

We hope that in this study, you have grown in your love and knowledge of Christ. Consider 1 John's opening statements, John spoke of what he had seen, heard, and touched. He wanted his audience to know the reality of the majestic, merciful, and magnificent God who is known through Jesus Christ. Consider for a moment as you close this study, who is your audience? Who has God placed around you who does not yet know in a deeply personal, loving way, the Lord Jesus Christ? Take time today to think on this, and then, as 1 John has taught us, love that person by taking action. Live in such a manner that your sin is repented of, and your good works are a credit to God's grace. Speak of Christ early and often to those who come to mind today. That which you have learned is not only for your blessing and benefit but for those around you who do not yet know the Lord.

We would love to hear how this study was useful to you in the Christian life. You can contact us with questions, comments, and encouragement at redeemingfamilypress@gmail.com

We would appreciate it if you could leave us a review on Amazon and share this study with your friends.

www.ingramcontent.com/pod-product-compliance
Lightning Source LLC
Chambersburg PA
CBHW060347050426
42449CB00011B/2859